y612.85 GRIB
Gribbin, Mary.
Hearing

JUN 3 0 '89

9.96

Hearing is about the exciting world of sound and how our ears receive information about life around us. The book looks at related issues such as the ways in which people can overcome defective hearing, the problem of noise pollution and the use of sound in modern technology.

© Macdonald & Co (Publishers) Ltd. 1985

First published in Great Britain in 1985
by Macdonald & Co (Publishers) Ltd
London & Sydney

A BPCC plc company

First published in the United States
in 1986 by Silver Burdett Company,
Morristown, New Jersey

LIBRARY OF CONGRESS CATALOGING IN PUBLICATION DATA

Gribbin, Mary.
    Hearing.

    Includes index.
    Summary: Discusses how our ears receive and trans-
late sound, deafness, noise pollution, and the use of
sound in modern technology.
    1. Hearing—Juvenile literature. [1. Hearing.
2. Sound]   I. Title.
QP462.2.G75   1986   612'.85   85-28161
ISBN 0-382-09173-6

faw

HEARING

Mary Gribbin

Silver Burdett Company
Morristown, New Jersey

How to use this book

First, look at the contents page opposite. Read the chapter list to see if it includes the subject you want. The list tells you what each page is about. You can then find the page with the information you need.

If you want to know about one particular thing, look it up in the index on page 31. For example, if you want to know about loudspeakers, the index tells you that there is something about them on page 22. The index also lists the pictures in the book.

When you read this book, you will find some unusual words. The glossary on page 30 explains what they mean.

Series Editor
Margaret Conroy

Book Editor
Valerie Hunt-Taylor

Production
Susan Mead

Picture Research
Suzanne Williams

Factual Adviser
Brian R. Ward

Reading Consultant
Amy Gibbs
Inner London Education Authority
Centre for Language in Primary
Education

Series Design
Robert Mathias/Anne Isseyegh

Book Design
Julia Osorno/Jane Robison

Teacher Panel
John Allen, Lynne McCoombe

Illustrations
Dave Eaton Front Cover
Ann Baum/Linda Rogers Associates
Pages 6-7, 10-11, 16-17, 20-21, 22-23, 24-25, 28-29
Lee Montgomery/Maggie Mundy
Pages 8-9, 12-13, 14-15, 19

Photographs
BPCC/Aldus Archive: cover top right and bottom left
Crown copyright, Building Research Establishment, photo reproduced by permission of the Controller, HMSO; 21
Sally and Richard Greenhill: cover top centre, 14, 20, 23
Fiona Pragoff: cover top left, 18 (photographed by courtesy of the Royal National Institute for the Deaf)
ZEFA: cover bottom right, 7, 25, 26, 27, 29

CONTENTS

HOW WE HEAR SOUND

What is sound?

Sound is made by air moving to and fro. If you pluck a guitar string you can see it vibrate, and you can hear the musical note it makes. But if you put your hand down flat on the string to stop the vibrating, the sound stops because the string is not pushing the air to and fro anymore. If you pluck the string gently, it makes a quiet note because the string only moves a little bit. If you pluck it harder, it pushes the air harder, so the vibrations are bigger, and that makes a louder noise.

Sometimes if you stand near a big pipe organ in a church while it is being played, your whole body can feel the air vibrate because the sound from the organ is so strong. Thunder can be so loud that it makes the windows rattle. But because air is transparent we cannot see the sound waves. They are invisible.

If you drop a stone into a pond, you will see ripples spread outward. Sound waves are a bit like ripples. They spread out in all directions.

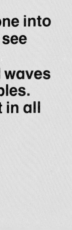

When sound waves reach your ear, they are funneled into the ear hole. Inside your ear, the vibrations in the air are turned into signals that pass along nerves to your brain. Your brain has to recognize what the signals mean. Babies don't know what the messages coming to their brains from their ears mean, until they learn what noise different things make. But you have learned the meanings of lots of different noises.

Music is vibrating air. A plucked guitar string makes the air vibrate. The vibration makes sounds in your ears.

Sound waves are invisible. But when the bell makes the air vibrate, your ear and brain know that it is time for recess.

Our ears

Sound waves travel into your ear along a short passage, like a tunnel. Inside, there is a thin tissue stretched across the passage. This forms the eardrum. It is joined to the first of three, tiny bones which are linked together. These are called the hammer, the anvil and the stirrup. Sound waves make the eardrum vibrate, and that makes the bones wiggle to and fro.

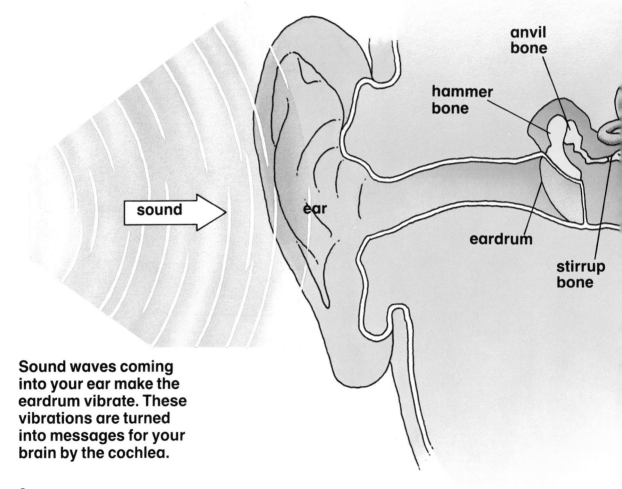

sound

ear

anvil bone

hammer bone

eardrum

stirrup bone

Sound waves coming into your ear make the eardrum vibrate. These vibrations are turned into messages for your brain by the cochlea.

8

Fluid inside the semi-circular canals swirls about when you move. This tells the brain which way up you are.

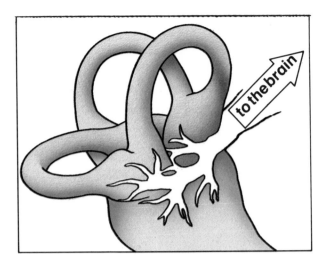

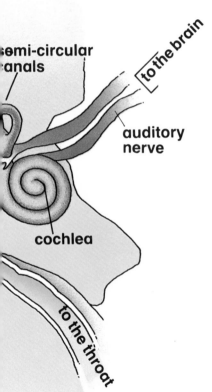

semi-circular canals

to the brain

auditory nerve

cochlea

to the throat

The bones in your ear join onto a tube that is wound up like a snail's shell, and is filled with fluid and very fine nerves. It is called the cochlea. The vibrations from the eardrum pass through the bones to the cochlea, and the auditory nerve carries news of the vibrations off to your brain.

But ears are not only for hearing. Inside your ear there are also three other tubes filled with liquid. They are called semi-circular canals, because of their shape. When you move your head, the fluid in these canals moves, and nerves inside them pass on messages to the brain. This is how your brain knows if you are moving, and works out how to keep your body balanced.

If you spin around very fast, the fluid in the canals gets in a spin. When you stop, the fluid continues to spin and your brain can't work out which way up you are, so you feel dizzy.

Why we need two ears

Both our ears work the same way. Even if you only had one ear that worked properly, you could still hear sounds and understand them. But having two ears helps us to find out more about what is going on around us. With two ears, we can tell which direction a sound is coming from.

Ears act as direction finders because sound arrives at one ear before it reaches the other ear. Your brain measures this difference and automatically works out the direction of the sound. Even very young babies turn to look in the direction a noise comes from.

As we grow up, we get better at figuring out where a noise is coming from and how far away the thing making the noise is. Sometimes this skill is called directional hearing.

Directional hearing was very important to our ancestors. They had to be able to track animals to hunt food. And, they had to know which way to run when large animals were tracking them.

Wild animals still need this skill today, and many of them have better directional hearing than we do. But directional hearing is still a very useful skill for us. If you heard someone shouting for help, you would know which way to run to get to them.

Sound waves reach one ear before the other. So your brain knows which way you should turn your head to see what is making the noise.

If you are hiding from a wild beast you have to keep very quiet. If you make a noise, the animal's directional hearing will tell it which way to run to catch you.

Animal hearing

Our ears work best at listening to sounds like people talking, or music, but animals have ears suited to different needs. Some animals can hear notes much higher than any sound your ears can hear, and others have ears that work best for listening to very deep notes. Some animals can hear faint noises, but others are completely deaf.

Snakes do not have ears at all, and people used to think they were deaf. But now we know that they can hear sounds through a bone that lies under the skin of their face. The bone vibrates when the air or the ground vibrates. This strange ear can only hear deep notes. Snakes really are deaf to high notes.

Animals such as dogs can move their ears without moving their heads. They can twitch them to and fro to find out where a sound is coming from.

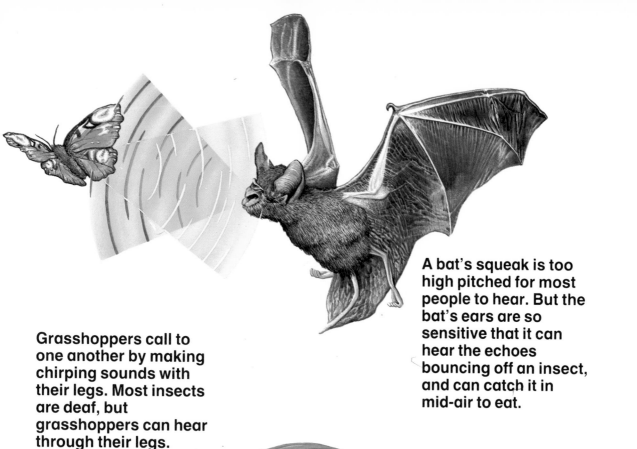

Grasshoppers call to one another by making chirping sounds with their legs. Most insects are deaf, but grasshoppers can hear through their legs.

A bat's squeak is too high pitched for most people to hear. But the bat's ears are so sensitive that it can hear the echoes bouncing off an insect, and can catch it in mid-air to eat.

Dogs can hear notes that are higher than those we hear. If you blow a special dog whistle that makes a very high note, you will not be able to hear it, but any dogs nearby will hear the note and might come running.

Sound isn't only useful for hearing. Some animals make high-pitched squeaking noises, too high for most people to hear. These squeaks bounce off nearby objects and make echoes, which the animal listens for. This is called echo-location. It is useful where there is little light to see, for example, underwater or at night. So dolphins use it to find their way about underwater; bats use it in the dark.

EAR AND BRAIN

Hearing and talking

When we speak we use our vocal chords to make the air vibrate. Vocal chords are rather like stretched elastic bands and lie in the voice box in your throat. If you put your fingers on the outside of your throat while you are speaking, you can feel the vibrations in your voice box. But the rest of your throat and mouth change the sounds that come out of your voice box. Each word is made a different way.

Try saying something and notice how your mouth moves differently to make each word.

Babies start by making noises like "ga ga" and "ma ma." But by listening to people they soon learn to join up the noises into words.

When we speak, we don't have to think about all the different ways we must use our lips, tongue, jaw, teeth and palate to make the sounds come out right. Only a very clever scientist can understand how your brain knows all the right things to do to make you speak. But even if you don't know any science at all, your brain is still clever enough to know what to do.

Speaking is as natural as walking. But we had to learn it once, just like learning to walk or ride a bicycle. Babies learn to talk by listening to the people around them and copying the noises they make. Next time you hear a baby making funny noises, think how much learning and practice it has to do before it can talk like you.

All the different parts of your throat and mouth work together to make the sounds we recognize as words.

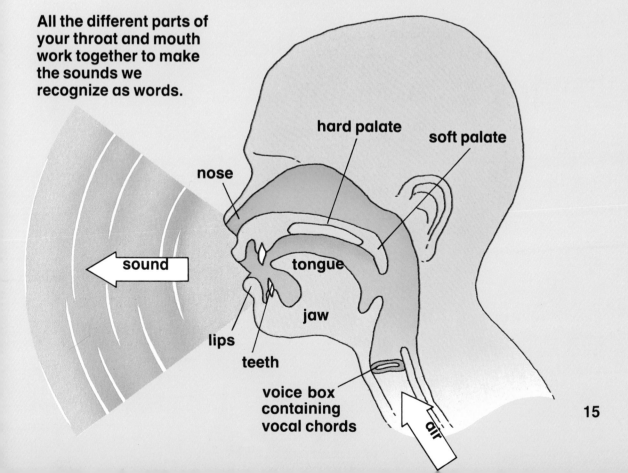

hard palate

soft palate

nose

sound

tongue

jaw

lips

teeth

voice box containing vocal chords

air

15

Listening

All the sound waves that get into your ears
make vibrations which are passed on to the
brain, as you saw on page 8. Starting when you
are very young, the brain learns what different
sounds mean. Once you had never heard the
sound of an ice cream truck playing a tune. Now
you know that when you hear the tune the truck is
coming and you might be able to buy some ice
cream. Perhaps you have seen a cat recognize
the sound of the can opener and know that it
means feeding time.

**Even in a room full of
noisy people talking,
a cat can pick out the
sound of a mouse.**

Sometimes your brain needs to ignore a lot of the sounds coming in through your ears. If lots of people are talking in the same room, you can concentrate on just one person and hear what he or she is saying. Sometimes you can be so interested in something you are doing, like reading a book, that you don't notice any of the sounds around you. Your brain is concentrating so hard that all the sounds are ignored. But at other times there can be so much noise that your brain can't ignore it.

Your brain is very good at picking out noises that it recognizes. If someone says your name, you will hear it leaping out at you, even on a busy playground where all the sounds are blurred together. Listening to a sound means much more than just hearing it. Do you listen to someone you find boring, or do you only hear the sounds they are saying?

It can be impossible to read in a room full of noise. All the messages coming into your brain from your ears may keep you from concentrating on your book.

17

Being deaf

Some people cannot hear sounds the way most of us hear them. They are deaf. Most deaf people do hear something, but what they hear is very faint or distorted. Their brains are working properly, but the messages coming from their ears are scrambled up. Being deaf can be very lonely, because it is difficult for people to talk to you.

If babies are born deaf, they cannot learn to speak the way other babies do. This is because they cannot hear the words other people are saying, so they cannot copy them. But there are other ways for deaf children to learn to speak. One way is by watching the pattern that their voice makes on a computer screen when they speak into a microphone.

Learning to speak using a computer. The teacher says a word first, and the deaf child practices until she can make a sound with a pattern which matches the pattern on the screen.

One form of sign language spells out letters of the alphabet by using the positions of your fingers.

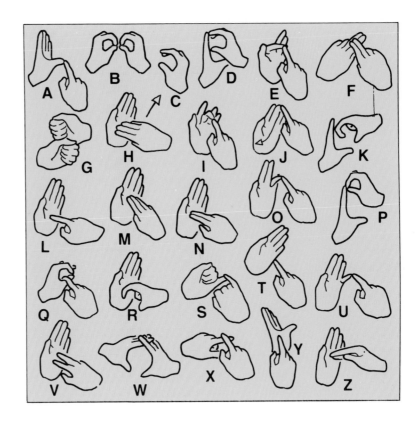

Another way deaf people communicate is by watching the lips of people speaking to them to work out what they are saying. When a deaf person has learned to speak, the words they say may sound strange. This is not because they are not clever, but because they cannot hear what they are saying.

Deaf people learn sign language so that they can talk to each other, and they try to learn to speak so that they can talk to us. But not many people who hear normally take the trouble to learn sign language. Are you clever enough to learn sign language? Try telling your friends a little story just by using finger spelling.

SOUNDS

Sound around us

Sound is all around us. It travels through water and through the ground as well as through air.

When you hear a sound coming to you from the room next door, it has traveled through the air, then through the solid wall, then through the air again before reaching your ear. But things that are very soft and squishy don't let sound through very well. If you put on a thick parka and pull the hood up over your ears, the padding in the hood muffles all the sounds.

If all the walls in your room were covered by something soft, they would muffle sounds too. Rooms which have to be kept free of sound from outside, like recording studios, have walls lined with cork or draped with curtains to keep sounds out.

Sound travels at 340 meters every second through air, and four times faster in water. Light travels much faster than sound. When there is a thunderstorm, you see a flash of lightning before you hear its sound (thunder). Thunder takes three seconds to travel every kilometer between you and the flash. So by counting the seconds between lightning and thunder you can work out how far away the flash was.

When fireworks explode, you see them flash before you hear their bangs. This is because light travels faster than sound.

20

We can use a decibel monitor to find out how many decibels of noise are being made by the traffic on this highway. If the noise is so loud that it measures over 120 decibels, it could damage our ears.

We measure sound in decibels. The faintest sound you could hear is 0 decibels; the loudness of your friend's voice talking to you is about 60 decibels. A busy street makes a noise of about 75 decibels.

Can you hear anything when you put your ear to the ground? Try listening in the middle of the park, or next to a soccer game.

Louder and softer

Sound is made by vibrating air. The bigger the vibrations are, the louder the noise is. We can muffle the sounds by putting our hands over our ears, or pulling up the hood of our parka. And we can get some peace and quiet by moving farther away from a noise, because the sound waves get weaker as they travel outward.

If you shout through a rolled up paper cone, the shout sounds louder and goes farther forward because all the sound waves are pushing in the same direction. But if a friend stands behind you while you are using the megaphone, they will think your voice is fainter. The megaphone stops the shout from spreading out around you.

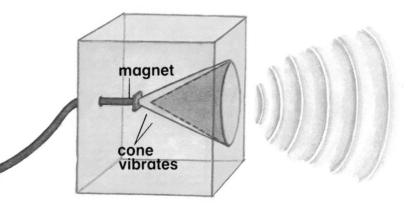

A rolled up paper megaphone pushes all the sound of your shout forward and makes it louder in front of you.

magnet

cone vibrates

Electrical signals push a magnet on the cone of a loudspeaker, to and fro. A big push makes a loud sound. A small push makes a quiet sound.

We can muffle the sound of a noisy road drill by putting our hands over our ears. Or we can muffle the sound by wrapping up the drill in a thick jacket. Which is the best way to keep the drill quiet?

A microphone can take quiet sounds and turn them into electrical signals which travel along wires to an amplifier and a loudspeaker. The amplifier makes the vibrations bigger, and uses them to push a magnet attached to a cone in the speaker. The magnet pushes the cone in and out. When we turn up the sound on a radio or record player, it makes the cone vibrate more. As the cone pushes the air harder, so the sound gets louder.

Pile cushions onto an alarm clock while it is ringing. What happens to the sound? Why? Now place the ringing clock on a metal tray and listen to what happens.

Warnings and signals

People living in cities don't need to listen for wild animals. But there are plenty of other warnings and signals that they get from their ears. Fire engines and school bells both make special noises that we know. Traffic sounds are important, and we all know to listen as well as to look when we cross the road. In some places blind people can cross the road safely at a pedestrian crossing thanks to the beeping sounds which tell when the traffic lights have turned red.

Sound can tell you if something is coming toward you or going away. A vehicle sounding a siren and rushing toward you pushes out sound waves close together, in front of it. The siren sounds high pitched. After it has gone past, the sound waves are stretched farther apart, behind, and make a deeper note. You can hear the note change as a police car or ambulance passes you.

The sound of breaking glass warns us that something is wrong. Because we have two ears we can tell which direction the sound is coming from, and run to get help if necessary.

As a high speed train goes past you, you will hear the sound it makes change from a high note to a deep note. This change in sound is called the Doppler effect.

What sounds can you recognize? Shut your eyes and try to describe what is going on around you to a friend. Think of all the different noises you use every day, from the sound of the alarm clock when it is time to get up, to the sound of someone's voice telling you it is time for bed.

Try making a tape recording of different noises, such as people talking, water pouring from a tap, street noises, or cornflakes being poured into a bowl. What other noises can you find to tape? Play the tape to your friends and see if they can guess what the sounds are.

Sound is more important in our lives than most people realize. The wind in the trees and all the warnings and signals, are just as important as listening to people talking.

Noise pollution

Sounds are very useful as warnings and signals, but when there is too much noise it makes life unpleasant. Our towns and cities are so full of people and traffic that we have to find ways to shut out the noise.

The level of sound in a quiet classroom will be only about 40 decibels and it will be easy to concentrate. But just one jet aircraft flying low overhead can make a noise as strong as 120 decibels, and you would find it very hard to work. People who have to live near airports, or near busy roads like highways, try to sound-proof their houses by fitting double glazing to their windows, and covering walls with soft materials like cork.

The sound coming through the loudspeakers at some concerts can be so loud that it can damage the hearing of people standing close to them.

Very strong sound waves damage the delicate parts inside our ears by making them vibrate more strongly than they ought to. People who work in noisy factories or shipyards, or out of doors at airports, need to wear earmuffs to protect their ears from the loud noise.

When ears are damaged by too much loud noise, they no longer respond to high pitched sounds or to faint sounds. Many musicians who have spent a long time playing in bands have damaged their hearing like this, because of standing close to their large loudspeakers.

But noise pollution doesn't only mean loud sound that damages your ears. Dirt and rubbish can spoil a pretty park for people who want to sit and enjoy it, and so can the sound from someone else's radio or cassette player if you are looking for peace and quiet.

The person guiding this helicopter in to land is wearing earmuffs to protect his ears from the loud noise of the helicopter.

Using sound

Echoes are heard when sound bounces off a hard surface like a wall. You can even bounce sound around corners in your home using a tin tray and a couple of homemade megaphones. But echoes are not just fun to play with. They are very useful for work.

Ships at sea can find out how deep the water is by bouncing sounds off the bottom. This is called echo-sounding, and helps ships to avoid big rocks that they might run aground on. Fishing boats also use echo-sounders to find shoals of fish.

If you prop a metal tray in the doorway and listen in its direction with a rolled up paper "ear trumpet," you can hear your friend whispering from around the corner through a megaphone.

On land, geologists can use echoes to find out what kind of rocks lie beneath the ground. They set off explosions on the surface of the ground, and detect sound waves which have traveled through the top layers of rock and bounced off different layers underneath. This helps geologists to find out which rocks hold oil.

Very high pitched sound, called ultrasound, can be used like X-rays to "see" inside things, Sound waves that pass through a piece of metal, or even a human body, change on the way through, and by measuring the changes scientists can make a picture of the inside.

Ultrasound is very important when doctors need to check if a baby is growing properly inside its mother. X-rays can be bad for a growing baby, but by using ultrasound the doctors can get a picture of the baby without hurting it. This is just one of the many useful ways in which scientists have made sound work for us.

By using an ultrasound scanner, doctors can see a picture of a baby before it is born and check that it is healthy.

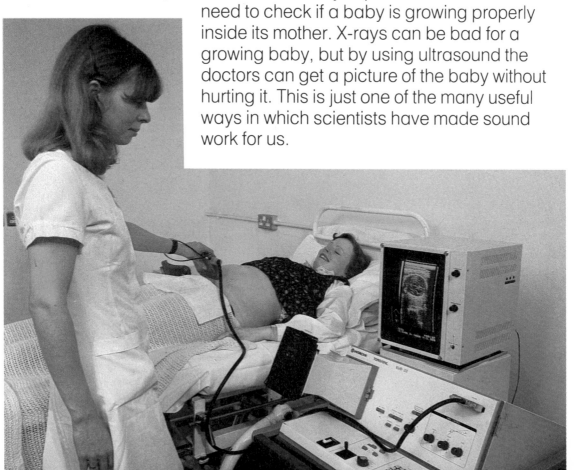

GLOSSARY, BOOKS TO READ

A glossary is a word list. This one explains unusual words that are used in this book.

Amplifier A machine that makes electric signals stronger, like those from a microphone.

Anvil One of three small bones in the middle of the ear that pass on sounds from the eardrum to the auditory nerve.

Auditory nerve A bundle of nerves which carry messages from each ear to the brain.

Cochlea The part inside the ear that turns sound vibrations into nerve messages that travel along the auditory nerve to the brain.

Decibel A unit used to measure sound.

Eardrum A thin piece of tissue inside your ear. It vibrates when sound waves reach it, and sends the vibrations on through three small bones to the inner ear.

Echo Sound which has bounced off a wall or some other surface and come back. You can often hear an echo when you shout or speak in a large, empty room.

Echo-location Bats make high pitched sounds which bounce echoes off things in front of them and back to their ears. This is echo-location. The bat uses echoes to locate things, the way we use our eyes to see.

Echo-sounding Using echoes made by bouncing sounds from a loudspeaker off the bottom of the sea to find how deep the water is.

Hammer The largest of the three small bones in the ear.

Loudspeaker A machine that turns electric signals into sound vibrations.

Megaphone A cone-shaped tube that you can use to make all the sound of your voice go forward. A megaphone can be made of metal or plastic, or just rolled up cardboard.

Microphone A machine which turns sound vibrations into electric signals. This is a bit like your ear turning sound into nerve signals.

Sign language A set of signs made with fingers that deaf people can use to "talk" to each other.

Stirrup Another one of the three bones inside the ear. It is shaped like a stirrup.

Ultrasound Sound which is so high pitched that human ears cannot hear it. Ultrasound makes very good echoes, for echo-location or echo-sounding, and it can also be used to look inside the human body.

BOOKS TO READ
You can find out more about hearing in these books.

The Story of Your Ear by Alvin Silverstein and Virginia B. Silverstein, Putnam Publishing Group, 1981.

Hearing by Ed Catherall, Silver Burdett, 1982.

The Ear and Hearing by Brian Ward, Franklin Watts, 1981.

Looking at the Senses by Nina Sully, David and Charles, 1982.

INDEX

The **dark** numbers tell you where you will find a picture of the subject.

Hammond Public Library
Hammond, Ind.

1 2 3 4 5 6 7 8 9 10—JDL—95 94 93 92 91 90 89 88 87 86